MW01196349

# You Don't Have to Marry the Wrong Man

# YOU DON'T HAVE TO MARRY THE WRONG MAN

## BY

## YVETTE HAYES

This book or any parts thereof may not be reproduced in any form, stored in a retrieval system, or transmitted in any form by any means-electronic, mechanical, photocopy, recording, or otherwise-without prior written permission of the publisher, except as provided by United States of America copyright law.

Unless otherwise noted, all Scripture quotations are from the King James Version of the Bible.

Copyright 2019-Yvette Hayes
All rights reserved by Walter Wardlaw, Jr. and Hester Wardlaw Publishing Company, LLC

*Disclaimer: The views and language in this book is solely of the author not Hester Wardlaw Publishing Company, LLC.*

*Disclaimer: I am not a professional marriage or relationship counselor. All information is solely based on my experiences and faith-based.*

# Contents

# Purpose

Many women are being murdered, abandoned, mishandled, and beaten by their husbands and boyfriends every day. Marriage and the dating process should never cause a woman to end up dead, abandoned, mishandled or beaten. However, these heart wrenching vicious cycles continue and I'm sick of it! I'm sick of attending funerals! I'm sick of lighting candles, I'm sick of hearing about these stories of our daughter's, sister's, grandbabies, cousins, aunties, and mothers having their lives ripped to shreds from a man who claims to love her.

My prayer and purpose are that after reading this book that not another woman will ever end up MARRYING THE WRONG MAN.

# Dedication & Special Recognitions

To my Mom and best friend, Lynn Mckoy Hayes, thank you for everything! It's because of you that I am who I am today. Rest in peace and I will see you in the morning. I love you mom.

I would like to dedicate this book to my granddaughter Danella Janay Harvey aka my "NannaBread", Big Guh, Chubbs, my great niece Kinsley Marie Lynn Sinclair aka "Munchkin" and may you girls never marry the wrong man.

# REMEMBERING MY GRANDMOTHERS.

Mrs. Viola Hayes

Thelma Mckoy Parker aka "Pete" &
Mrs. Inez Nealey

Luvenia Williams Hayes

A special thank you to my HERO and the strongest man I know. If he ever ran for President, he would have my vote, my Dad William Douglas Hayes. I love you and thank you for always believing in me. I will continue to always do the right thing. To my step-mom Mrs. Mary Hayes, I love you and thank you for being an exemplary role model. To my sister Connie, you are so intelligent, I love you and thank you for always supporting me. To my daughter, Shalonda, be encouraged and thank you for listening to me read each chapter to you repeatedly. I thank God for choosing me to be your mother. You have brought so much joy to my life and I love you. To my brother Willie, I'm so happy to have you for a brother. To my nephew Jarrad aka Noot-Noot, you are such a kind and selfless man and one day you're going to make a great husband/dad.

Special thanks to the best church in North Carolina, New Light Apostolic Church of Jesus Christ, founder the late Bishop Donald Todd and now my Pastor Bobbi Todd. I love you all and thank you for all your prayers and support!

I almost forgot to say thank you to my YouTube family, thank you all for your love and support. It's because of you guys that I'm "Livin my best life".

To all of you that I didn't name that have prayed for me and believed in me, thank you and to God be the glory.

# My Story

On December 28th, 1970, God gave me to Mr. William Douglas Hayes and Lynn McKoy Hayes. Contrary to what my siblings Connie and Kenny would tell you, I'm sure this was the best day of my parent's life. I would like to say that I grew up in a wonderful home. My parents were not perfect, but they did what was best for their children and for that, I tell God thank you!

Like most young girls growing up, I couldn't wait to start dating, ready to be grown and on my own. I was so ready to get out of my parent's house. They were always telling me what I could and couldn't do. I had to be in the house before the street lights came on...ugh...rules, rules, and rules.

Later in life, I would come to realize that they had set rules and boundaries for my protection, because they loved me and only wanted what was best for me. So on with my story, at the age of seventeen, I found myself pregnant with no husband only a boyfriend who was very abusive. I had my first child at the age of eighteen. I continue to date and cohabitate with her father who continued to be abusive and later burned my apartment down. From that relationship, I went on to date other men who had all types of problems and challenges as well. Dysfunction was all I knew when it came to relationships. I didn't know that a man was to be my provider, protector and friend. I didn't even know my own worth, I was somebody and I mattered. I would go on to have another child by the age of twenty-one. Still not married, a single mother who had given birth to two children with different fathers living in the projects. So, I'm not a novice when it comes to dating the wrong men. Though I've never been married, God, experiences, and life has taught me who NOT to marry. I really believe that what we go through in life is to help somebody else. I have been through many challenges in life. I believe that since God has allowed me to survive and be here, it is my duty to share what I have learned. Today, I can stand boldly and proclaim that by the grace of God, I have been made whole!

# Intro:

# You are Somebody

You are somebody.  Did you know that?  Well, if you didn't you do now.  You were created by the almighty God, who has never ever made a mistake.  I don't care how you got here.  Rather it was through rape, incest, by way of a one-night stand or an "I do" commitment at the altar, you are somebody and you matter.  Did you hear what I said?  Come a little closer and let me say it a little louder.  YOU ARE SOMEBODY!

You may be five or seventy-five, dark skinned, light skinned, overweight, underweight, educated, or not so educated, ramen noodle feed or fillet mignon served. It does not matter; the truth and the whole truth is you are somebody. You deserve to be treated well and you deserve to marry well.

You are a female, a lady, a girl, a woman. You are the only creation of God that is compatible with a man. More precious than diamonds more valuable than a Rolls-Royce with a trunk full of Birkin bags, oh yes and don't you ever forget it.

You are not a mistake. There is nothing wrong with you. You never have to compare yourself to another female. You are just beautiful, just as capable and just as worthy than any other female. Trust me when I tell you, "What God has for you is for you". In this life you are going to have trials and tribulations. You are going to even make one or two maybe even three bad decisions but keep on living. Keep on moving up. Never settle and don't take any wooden nickels. You are a Kings daughter. You can't be bought, and you will not strip. Never apologize for knowing your worth. You are good enough, amazing, intelligent and a giver of life. Be you and live your best life because you are somebody and you will marry the right man.

# 1

# The Abusive Man

When His Fist Meets Your Eye

*Proverbs 22:24(KJV) "Make no friendship with and angry man; and with a furious man thou shalt not go"*

Every day in the US more than three woman are murdered by their husbands or boyfriends. Every nine seconds a woman is assaulted or beaten. These facts are very disturbing and yet everyday women are dating and marrying abusive men. Why? Well, I'm glad you asked; Why would a women date or marry an abusive man? No woman wakes up and says…..." I sure hope

I meet and marry a man that's going to blacken my eye". No parent raises their daughter to go out and marry a man that will physically abuse them. These are not our goals. The abusive man is not whom mama and daddy had vision for our lives. So, the question is still at hand. Why do we end up with an abusive man? How do we determine if we are dating an abusive man who does not know how to process his anger?

There are many red flags, but I will try and make it plain in reviewing three of these red flags. Number one, if you are reading this book right now and your eye is black from his fist meeting your eye then that is one red flag or indication that the man you are dating has a problem with processing his anger.

Number two, if he has choked you, kicked you, spit on you, called you out of your name, wouldn't let you leave the house or threaten you, then you are dealing with an abusive man. Finally, number three is one of the biggest yet at the same time may seem small. It is the abuse of control. If a man must control every aspect of your life… what did you eat, where did you eat, where you're going and how long you're going to be gone, so on and so forth, be very careful ladies. Control is a subtle type of abuse that leads to more abuse and more tragedies to be read or heard on the evening news. It is not the will of God for you to be abused. Rather it be physical, verbal, emotional or mental abuse. All abuse is abuse and is unacceptable. Don't take any form of abuse lightly. You can not change an abusive man. He has not been sent to you from God for you to rehabilitate. You are not the anger management counselor.

I was reading an article in a magazine one day and this lady was sharing her story about how her husband had shot and killed her two small children then killed himself. This story as well as many others like it is a tragedy. Pay attention to the red flags while dating. Don't ignore your conscience and don't ignore the Holy Spirit. He knows who you should be joined with in marriage and an abusive man is not the man you should marry.

It is in the early diagnosis of the relationship that will help you determine the future health of your marriage. A house is only as strong as the foundation it was built upon and a marriage is only as strong as the overall health of the individuals. Therefore, ladies be diligent and be sober! Pay attention to this man's actions and not just his words.  Pay attention to his treatment of others and most definitely pay attention to his treatment of you!  You don't have to be hospitalized.  You don't have to come home to the death of your children.  You don't have to be the next victim with another victim story and most importantly you don't have to marry an abusive man.

# 2

# You Can't Change Insanity

*John 10:20 (KJV), "And many of them said, He hath a devil, and is mad; why hear ye him?*

Ladies listen, listen, listen as a matter of fact, if you are standing up sit down. Let me tell you something and let me be perfectly clear. You cannot change insanity. You know what, that's not how I wanted to say it. Due to the high rate of women being murdered everyday by their husbands and boyfriends I'm going to say this; "YOU

CAN'T CHANGE CRAZY"! That's right I said it, C-R-A-Z-Y, CRAZY! When you meet a man and his criminal record is longer than two football fields, his mom is afraid of him and when his previous wife or girlfriend has a restraining order against him for life then these facts mean that this person is crazy-problematic. You can't change him. Lay your hands on yourself and repeat after me. I can't change him. I don't care how many gifts you buy him. I don't care how submissive you have become. You may have even isolated yourself from all your family and friends. Guess what it's still not enough. He will not change. He's still going to accuse you of cheating. He's still going to tell you that you think you are smarter and better than him. You can put on a dress down to your ankles and he's still going to tell you that you look like a "garden tool". He will continue to beat you repeatedly. Why? I'm glad you asked. It's because the way this man thinks, and processes information is on another level. Now, what can you do with that? NOTHING! Being nice is not going to change him. As a matter of fact, let me tell you about "nice". Nice is in the grave. Nice has been shipped back to her family in a box. The scripture says, "why listen to him?' You can't rehabilitate him; you can't love him to wellness. You can't unscramble the eggs. Don't get involved with this type of man. Let somebody else be his savior, preferably Jesus Christ.

ו

# 3

# The Married Man

# (He is not your husband)

*Matthew 19:6b (KJV), "What therefore God hath joined together, let not man put asunder."*

There can be two types of married men. The married man that the single woman hopes will one day leave his wife and marry her. Then there is the married man that just wants to spend time with the single woman. So, let's begin with the single women who has hopes and dreams of one day becoming the married man's wife.

Now for most of us we know we can't marry a married man. Why the dreaming single woman may ask? Well, because he is already somebody else's husband. He's already been to the altar. He's already put a ring on someone else's finger. He's living in a house with someone else and raising children. You would think that these facts would cancel out all hopes and dreams of a married man becoming your husband. For some women they feel like they have gotten a revelation from God that this man has married the wrong woman. Listen to me ladies, if you have got the heart of your eye balls set on someone else's husband then me, the Lord and seventeen angels are writing this book to tell you that your eye balls will melt out of their sockets before this married man becomes your husband. Now someone may beg to differ and say... "Well I married a married man and we been together for thirty-five years and all is well". Now this may be true, and all may be well now, but let's not leave out parts of the testimony. For the first twenty-five years of you being married to the married man you had to deal with fifteen other women, seventeen outside children and countless harassing phone calls. No wife wants to endure this kind of pain in her marriage. Guess what ladies you don't have too, if you choose right. You can never get right out of wrong and you can never get wrong out of right. Desiring a married man will always be wrong. I don't care if this man has married a woman with three heads and five arms. It is still his wife and God honors marriage. Therefore, I would strongly suggest that you get another dream and another hope because a married man is not your husband.

Now onto the next married man. The married man that wants to spend time with the single woman. Ladies if there is a married man that is showing you some interest the best thing for you to do is to nip it in the bud. Once you find out that this man has a wife it should be a wrap. Don't entertain the married man's conversation in any kind of way. It doesn't matter how bad he tells you his wife treats him. It doesn't matter how much weight he says his wife has gained. It doesn't matter how bad he says her food taste. Having you will not fix his issues with his wife. Neither will having you make him a better man. If he is cheating on his wife, he will be cheating on you. His issues are not with his wife, but his issue is with his character. If he needs someone to talk to let him go and talk to his pastor. If he needs someone to be sweet and kind to let him go be sweet and kind to his mother.  If he just needs someone to take a stroll around the park with let him go walk his dog.  You can never repair or change a man's character.  You may be a different woman than his wife.  His wife may speak loudly.  You may speak soft.  His wife may open a can of food to cook it.  You may make the food from scratch.  None of these things matter because the character of a man is not based on how well he is treated by the wife or the mistress.  I know plenty of women and you do too, that have cooked, cleaned and look the part.  All to have their husband still have an affair.  Having an affair with a married man is nothing to be proud of.  It is the devils' job to paint a pretty picture, but affairs only lead to three things.  These three things are shame, guilt and regret.  The Bible clearly says that the wages of sin is death.  We all know of people who have lost their lives because of an affair.  It is so important what type of man we start out with.  If we start out with Sally Sues husband trust and believe within the next five years, he will be Mary Sues husband too.  Changing marriage beds will not change a man's character condition.  It will not change the fact that he already has a wife.  I'm going to end this by stating one simple fact and that is that all married men are unavailable to you.  It is alright to have your own man.  It's alright to not be the side piece or the rebound chic.  You don't have to destroy another woman's home by secretly having an affair with her husband.  God knows what you like and what is best for you.  Have some integrity about yourself and refuse to be another man's dumping ground.  Let's make marriages great again and send him home to his wife.

# 4

# The Jobless Man

# (If I can just help him get

# on his feet)

*Proverbs 21;25 (KJV), The desire of the slothful killeth him; for his hands refuse to labor. "*

Allow me to explain something to you. If I had a dollar for every time, I made that statement…. "If I can just help him get on his feet", I would be the richest woman in the world. I had a friend that I would tell this to all the time, and she would say,

"Yvette you have been saying this for years about this same man". "All I want to know is what is wrong with his feet?" We would laugh so hard about that statement. So, I ask you ladies this same question if you are dating a jobless man; what is wrong with his feet? More than likely nothing is wrong. His feet are fine, his hands are fine, and nothing is wrong with his eye balls. He can see. The problem doesn't lie within his physical abilities. The problem lies within four letters. Repeat this after me… L-A-Z-Y. Simply put, he is lazy with no desire to work. The Bible refers to this as slothfulness.

The jobless man doesn't want to take on any responsibilities. He doesn't want to work. He doesn't want to pay any bills, cut grass, and do maintenance on your car. If you have a flat tire, call him, see if he responds. More than likely you will get no response because something is wrong with his feet and you are still operating on them.

The jobless man refuses to work or labor for an honest wage so that he can sustain his family. This is a hazardous situation to your health ladies. The Bible says that a man that doesn't take care of his household is worse than an infidel (*1 Timothy 5:8*). It goes on to say that if a man doesn't work, he doesn't eat (*2 Thessalonians 3:10*). So, in other words if you choose a man to marry that doesn't care nothing about buying grocery, I promise you that marriage will have problems.

The big question is why do women marry and support lazy slothful men? Now I'm not talking about a man that has a good working history that may have been injured on the job. Nothing is wrong with a man in this situation.  I'm referring to the man who is in good health and nothing is wrong with him.  Why do women form relationships and marry these types of men?  Now this may sound harsh but I'm going to say this, there is nothing attractive about a man who has no money and can't handle business.  It doesn't matter how good he smells or how good he looks.  His eyes can change color with the seasons.  When the utility bill comes in the mail his physical appearance goes out the window.  We're going to need some money to keep the lights on.

There is a big misunderstanding of a man's position and a woman's position in a marriage.  The position of the man is to be the provider for his family.  Ladies when you are choosing a husband he should be in the position or right at the door of the position as a good provider.  It is not your position to provide for him. We all know of women and I have been one of them who are taking care of men. You may be working the forty hour a week job, paying all the bills, buying the bacon and cooking it too. Then to top it all off he may be taking you to work in your car and dropping you off. Then he comes back late to pick you up because he's been hanging out with the boys and Sally Sue. My God this should not be! He is a man, and men understand the role as a provider. A real man would never place you in a position of a provider while he kicks back and does nothing. Young ladies it is in the early stages of a man's life that he learns to be responsible and the benefits of honest work. So, make sure you pay attention to a young man's attitude towards hard work and his current responsibilities. Seasoned ladies, when a man is between the age of thirty and above with no current job, when he hasn't worked anywhere within the past five years, but had a job sitting down and stood up and got fired (in the words of my auntie) then this is a big issue that can't be ignored. When you meet a man, and this is his pattern for work just know that marriage will not change his pattern or attitude towards finding and keeping a job. You don't want to be married and bear the financial burden of a household alone. You are not Job Link. You are not part of the Labor Ready Board. You are not this man's mother. Don't fall into a pity party and don't fall into any emotional trap. Your decision to not have a jobless man for your husband does not make you arrogant. However, it does make you a woman who has chosen to wait on a responsible man who knows how to provide for his family.

# 5

# The Porn Addict

"You are no match for the Vixen"

Pornography acts like a drug in the brain and it is just as addictive yet even more powerful as crack cocaine. Once you're hooked, you're hooked. It is a million-dollar industry. You will most definitely need an intervention from God.

The good Lord created sex. I know He did, because anything that is good must have come out of the mind of God. Sex was created to be enjoyed between a man and a woman in the confines of marriage. Today man has perverted sex and has changed a good thing into something immoral. It appears everybody is taking their clothes off with no shame. People today want to have sex with as many people as possible at the same time. They don't mind sharing and watching one another. Some have even decided to have open marriages which allow as many folks as possible to visit their marriage bed. Men who watch porn can't get enough and you will not be able to satisfy them. There are married women today who must compete with the vixen on the screen. Many husbands want to watch porn while being intimate with their wives. Some even prefer the vixen on the screen over their own wife. They will even try to make their wives do what they have seen on the screen. Their appetite has become perverted and casual

Yvette Hayes

sex with their wife isn't so casual or exciting anymore. Intimacy has become filled with all kinds of lewd and lascivious acts. Baby when I tell you, you are no match for the vixen you must believe it. You will be surprised what these men like to do in private. Don't get me wrong I understand that the marriage bed is private, and you can do what you like, but there are still some boundaries. Because like we said earlier God created sex to be enjoyed between a man and a woman, not five different folks, two blow-up dolls and a 27-inch tv screen displaying other people's sexual encounters. Men have become so perverted, abnormal and unhealthy in their minds that they can't even imagine having pleasure from being intimate with only their wife.

While dating you had better talk about something other than what size house you will have and who you want for your neighbors. You must find out this man's sexual appetite, because as ladies we're not going to be able to perform everything at a man's request. That's why it is so imperative that we marry the right man. If he tells you he enjoys watching porn that would be a red flag. If he shares with you that he doesn't mind inviting other folks to the bedroom that would be a red flag to stop processing his application immediately. You can not change his appetite for porn. I don't care how much weight you lose. I don't care how high the stilettos may be. You can jump from pillow to post it doesn't matter. A person addicted to crack cocaine can spend the entire night getting high, once he wakes up the first thing he will want is some more crack cocaine. It is an addiction which has affected the brain and a man who has developed a habit of viewing porn is no different. The more porn he views the more he will want to view and being married to you will not change that.

No wife wants to have her husband's body while his mind is finding more pleasure in the images that have been embedded in his brain by way of viewing pornography. You don't have to marry a man that is addicted to porn. You can choose. The good news is that there are many men who have healthy sexual appetites who have not allowed their brains to be corrupted with pornography. He will desire to be intimate with only you, that's right only you. No extra people, no blow-up dolls and no videos to be viewed. You will be enough, be patient and wait.

# 6

# Looking for Love at the State Penitentiary

There is a catastrophic number of black men locked up here in these United States of America. Some deserving and some not so deserving. Some men only must have one sound of those doors closing behind them, to figure out that this life is not for them, while others it may take a lifetime. Then there are some who wouldn't have it any other way they love prison life.

Ladies I understand that we all just want to be loved by that perfect man who will protect and provide for us. We all want it. There is nothing wrong with wanting love and a husband. This is the will of God. We must never throw caution to the wind whenever we seek a husband from the state penitentiary. Let me start by telling my own business. I have dated men in prison and men straight out of prison. Them jokers had some challenges you hear me. You never can really see the challenges while they are locked up. Because one thing about being in prison you can get an early release for good behavior. So, for the most part, they behave well. They are the best poets, the best artist, and they will tell you everything you want to hear. Nobody couldn't tell me God didn't send this man to prison just to be found by me. God has answered my prayers and so what he's in prison. This man is good to me, so I thought.

Ladies let me ask you something. What else can he be? He's in a controlled environment. Do you think he is going to slap you in front of the officers and get his stay extended? I think not. Before I go any further let me say this. All men that are in prison are not dangerous. There are some men who have been to prison or jail that have come out to be great men in society. These men can be wonderful role models and they can make great husbands. However, you better make sure that this man has just made a bad choice at one point in his life and this is not who he really is.

So, let's consider a few truths when choosing men in prison. Truth #1: If this man is forty-five with a history of being in and out of some type of behavior facility since he was ten years old, what are you going to do to keep him from going back to prison?  His problem is bigger than your consistent visits, bigger than the money you keep on his books and bigger than the home you may provide for him when he gets released.  Can somebody say, "Bigger"?  From ten to forty-five in and out prison, you are wasting your time.  History is so important, it tells "his" story.  You never choose a man whom you must fix and build.  You don't sign up to be wife only to start counseling sessions for your husband.  If this man has lived a consistent life in and out of prison, you can forget it.  Who told you that you are supposed to take this position, to suffer and be the wife of a man who can't stay out of prison.  Many of us take these positions with no marriage license at all.   It is not your responsibility to raise a grown man.  With no shame and with no guilt move on and stop living a life of dysfunction. Dysfunction is to deviate from the norm. The norm is that parents are to raise children. Men are to lead their families to a place of wellness, not prison. Tell God thank you right there!

Truth#2: This is something that no one likes to talk about but I'm going to write about it. Sex in prison, that's right, men are having sex in prison. Most men while in prison must compromise their sexuality. Some men are raped, and some men are willing, while others may have to fight and stand there ground not to compromise. However, this is a truth that you will have to deal with. Now will he tell you. Probably not, some men who have spent some time behind bars come out very angry along with being easily aggravated. You with your good sweet self can't understand why this

man is always mad at the world. Well;
could it be because he is trying to process
some inward turmoil? Some turmoil that he
can't even speak about, being raped by
another man or living a life of going alone to
get alone just to live. Now what are you
going to do with that ladies? What save do
you have for that? None.........

Final truth to consider, this man has
been locked up for some period. Do you
think it is in your best interest as well as his
best interest to enter a marriage? He's been
in a structured and controlled environment
for the past however many years it has been.
He hasn't had to lead, he hasn't had to pay
bills, he hasn't had to provide or be
responsible for anyone besides himself. He
hasn't been faced with the challenges that
come with living in the outside world.
Days, months, and years have passed by

while he has been in prison. We all know that this world changes from day to day. He's going to need a chance to get back into the swing of things and put some shoes to those feet to walk out all his promises. He's going to need time to prove himself. If your child has been diagnosed with a serious illness you wouldn't just trust the words of a family friend to let their grandmother prescribe and treat your child because she cured everybody's cold in the family. No, you would have to see some credentials. You would want to see some proof that this person has been through the proper training and is credible. Home remedies are good for some situations but not for my child's life. Same is true with who you marry. Let this man prove himself first. We must not forget that while locked up you were his favorite flavored chocolate ice cream. Now there are vanilla, strawberry, sherbet, and butter pecan. I'm just saying, it would be wise not to marry this man in prison or straight out of prison. If he proves to be a man who is ready to lead a family, happy trails to you. If he turns out not to be the man who is ready to lead a family still happy trail to you also. It will be a win-win for you either way. Just a few things to consider while down at the state penitentiary looking for love.

# 7

# Know them by their Fruit

If a man is claiming to be a Christian, there are certain things he will not compromise, and he will not persuade you to compromise either.  As we all know sex is the hot topic that is on everybody's mind.  Seems like everyone is doing it and if they aren't doing it, they want to do it.  God has created this beautiful thing called sex to happen within the confines of marriage.  Don't let no man tell you he must test drive the car before he drives it.  That is all well and fine at the Ford dealership.  You are a human being, not a car.

Being a Christian woman myself, sometimes it can be very discouraging trying to find Mr. Right in the church. On Sunday morning everyone is on their best behavior, presenting their best selves. Just like a first date can be. When a man attends church frequently, we automatically believe that he is a good old saved man. He may teach Sunday school, drive the church van, preach the sermon, know how to dance before the Lord, and may even be the most faithful in giving his money. Sounds like a winner doesn't it? Or is he really? Don't get me wrong ladies all these things are good but look a little deeper because if I can recall to my memory, we had a few serial killers who served just as well.

The fact that a man attends church and he may even say with his mouth that he is a Christian doesn't mean he is one. You ever heard the saying "action speaks louder than words"? I'm sure you have heard that before. So, when we are choosing a man to marry, we must observe more than his words and his actions in a controlled environment. We must spend time with him and observe his character. Character is who he is when nobody is watching. It is who he is in his private life.

I dated a man once who told me he was a Christian and wanted to take me on a date. So, of course, I agreed to go on this date, I was so excited. I got myself dressed looking all cute and everything. Ready to go was I, so we go on our date. We went to the movies then out to eat dinner. We went to the mall with no shopping just conversating the whole time. It begins to rain, it was getting late, so headed back to the house. We took highway 95 back.

Now, ladies, I want to you to read closely what I am about to say to you. Now, in the beginning, I told you this man told me that he was a Christian if you remember. So, as we are riding along and the rain was coming down. It was getting dark outside also. Do you know what this man has the nerve to ask me? He asks me would I like to go to the motel and stay over for the night. You see what I'm saying, ladies, we must be careful because there are so many different strands of Christians. Like the HIV virus, there are different strands of men. We don't want men that don't practice having restraints. We want men that know how to keep their clothes on before marriage. This is important, marriage will not cure lust. It will also not cure fornication or adultery. If you marry a man that will offend God and sleep with you before marriage, I promise you it's going to be very difficult to keep him faithful after the vows are exchanged. Lust is a very powerful thing especially when one is out of control. It has been known to burn down many marriages.

Ladies we want to make the best choice for a quality Christian husband. Now if you are not into Christianity you can marry whomever you like but I want a good born-again Christian man since I am a Christian woman. Tell God thank you right there! The standards of Christianity seem to be alright with me because of the author and finisher. You know his name, Jesus Christ. Alright, let me get back to writing because at the mention of his name I feel my help coming on now!

The Bible tells us we can know them by their fruit ladies and a Christian man will not try to get you in the bed before marriage. Every man must know how to rule his own body well. Let me tell you why ladies. You see when we get married we are not going to be doing all the grocery shopping. Our husbands will be visiting the local Walmart, Save-a-Lots, and Seven Elevens. They will be visiting these stores just to pick up a jug of milk and guess who else will be picking up a jug of milk. Bad body, half naked, big butt Sally Sue is going to be in the same store picking up a jug of milk also. I'm sure she likes cereal too. You see here lies the problem ladies. We sent our Jim Bob to pick up a jug of milk. Not to get syphilis, gonorrhea, outside children or Sally sue. If you choose to marry a man who doesn't have the capacity to follow a simple grocery list, come home without flirting, and creating outside relationships with other women your marriage will be in trouble. We want to choose a man that loves God and respects us as his wife enough to be able to speak to Sally Sue, purchase the milk, then come home in that order. Your husband will not only be interacting with women at the grocery store, but he will be interacting with your sisters, your cousins, your aunties, co-workers and even your mother. If he will chunk Christian morals out the window and take his pants off before marriage with you then more than likely Christian morals will not be the flashing red light that keeps him from having an affair.

I have been living for some years now and I have never seen an apple tree produce oranges. This world is full of hypocrisy. People proclaiming to be one thing in public but in private they are something opposite. This is your life and you must pay attention in order to recognize when someone is fake.

We have the right to marry whomever we choose. If you are a witch, I'm sure you want to marry a warlock. If you are an atheist, I'm sure you want to marry an atheist. We all want to be with like-minded people. This doesn't mean that you will choose a carbon copy of yourself. We do want to choose someone who at least stands on the same foundations. If a man says he is a Christian, there is a certain way we should expect him to carry himself in public and in private. As Christians, we live according to the scriptures by the grace of God.

So, ladies if you are dating a man that claims to be a Christian and he's trying to get you to make footprints in the ceiling before marriage he isn't the best choice. Christian men who aren't married don't commit fornication. They will not persuade you to commit fornication. The worst thing I'm sure to find out later, is that on the wedding night you laid down with a prince to end up waking with a frog. People are not what they say but what they do. He can claim Christian all day long, but if his life in public and private dictates otherwise he isn't the one. Every place of business has a code of standards and the life of a Christian does too. Don't be discouraged and wait patiently for that genuine Christian man. God has plenty of men that will not compromise. Men that will not tell you that it's okay to have sex before marriage because we are engaged. Don't let social media fool you. Everybody isn't messing around. God has plenty of men who are what they say they are. When he presents himself to you, you will know him by his FRUIT.

# 8

# The Man on the D.L.

# (Down Low)

This chapter starts off by asking for your prayers. I don't want to end up in jail for what I'm about to write. This is not any hate speech. This chapter is dedicated to women who don't want to be deceived by a gay man. If a man chooses to be gay, he has that right. God gives us all a free will. However, there are some of us ladies who don't choose to be married to a man on the down low. We have the same right. To the men if you are a man on the D.L. please give that woman the right to choose if she wants to be married to a gay man or not. Don't conceal it from her. Marrying a woman will not stop you from being gay.

A man on the D.L. (down-low) is a man who in public seemingly appears to be a straight man, but in private he enjoys having sexual relationships with other men. Now ladies let me tell you something right here. You would have thought that you had a bad day if you came home and caught your husband in bed with Sally Sue. Just imagine if you came home and caught your husband in the bed with Billy Bob. A bad day would be turned into doomsday.

There are so many men who are hiding their sexuality for so many different reasons. I'm not here to write about all the reasons but I will say this. Some men will use your hand in marriage as a cover-up. These men want to cover up the fact that they are gay. Just because a man is married doesn't mean that he is not gay. Some men will propose to you, meet you at the altar, and let you have their children all while having a full blown out sexual relationship with another man. That's why it is so important that you don't go into a marriage if you have low self-esteem. Low self-esteem is just like a bleeding wound and the lions can smell your injury. This will cause them to pounce on you. I stay encouraged and help to keep other big women and girls encouraged. The stereotype is that big girls and women have low self-esteem. We are just happy to be picked by a man. The devil is a liar! It doesn't matter if you are big, fat or fluffy, we will wait on the right man to marry.

There are so many women who are married to gay men right now and seem to be clueless. Ladies when a gay man is involved with another man, he does the same things that a straight man would do. For example, why is it that no matter when his "homebody" calls he will get up to go check on him? Six am, noon or midnight, when this man calls your fiancé or husband, he quickly leaves you to run to him. I don't care if they were childhood friends. The Bible says when you were a child you did like a child but now that you are a man you should do as a man. I wish my husband would have a cycle of getting up out of our bed at midnight to go check on his "homeboy"! Why do all his "homeboys" seem to be so feminine? I believe if you are a man you should act like a man. The real petite ladies, some of you don't even have to shop for your own clothes because your fiancé or husband enjoys picking out your clothes more than you do, this is because he gets pleasure out of dressing how he would like to dress through you. These are just a few questions and observations to consider. We live in a very selfish world with a lot of selfish people. The Bible says in *Jeremiah 17:9* that the heart is deceitful above all things, and desperately wicked. Who can know it?

You better make sure you know who you are marrying. When you enter marriage everything that was once only yours now becomes one hundred percent accessible to your husband. He is now one hundred percent accessible to your home to your finances and to your body. Statistics prove that HIV is more prevalent in the gay community. A man on the D.L. will marry you fully aware that he has HIV and won't reveal it to you until you become sick and you can't figure out why your health is failing.  Now you may say I'm not signing up for that.  Take full responsibility for your life.  You must recognize that you deserve the best.  Taking full responsibility means that when a man asks you to marry him it is your responsibility to request a health examination.  That is your right to ask.  Never judge a man by the M.D. in front of his name, by his bank account, and by what comes out of his mouth.  You better judge him by some receipts.  What do you see?  I've always been told that if it walks like a duck and quakes like a duck then baby you can go ahead with calling him Donald.

You had better pay attention and ask some questions ladies.  I don't care how many muscles he has.  I don't care about how many babies he wants or how bad he talks about the gay community. It doesn't matter if he quotes scriptures. When someone is trying to hide something from you, you must become your own inspector gadget. Pay attention to this man's behavior. Men have a certain way that they carry themselves around the people that they are intimate with whether it's male or female. I don't want to hear another female say, "I didn't know he was gay." If you can take the time to research and spend the money to make sure you are buying authentic hair and not synthetic hair you can most definitely take the time to make sure you are not marrying a man on the D.L.

# 9

# The Man with no Fixed Time

*Proverbs 18:22 (KJV), "Whoso findeth a wife findeth a good thing, and obtaineth favour of the Lord."*

Younger Self: "Hey Mrs. Lou Ella, I finally got engaged."

Mrs. Lou Ella: "When is the wedding date?"

Younger Self: "I don't know but it's coming."

Mrs. Lou Ella: "Jesus and Christmas are too…"

When I was a little girl, I can remember my mom coming home with baskets full of snap peas and butter beans. This would mean only one thing for me and my siblings. We would not be going out to play until we shelled all those snap and butter beans. Once we finished this tedious job of shelling and fussing with each other over who shelled the most beans my mom would not cook them right away. She would take the beans and put them in a freezer bag and store them away in the deep freezer to be eaten at a much later date. My mom loved storing beans. She did this every year. They were never meant to be eaten right away always for later use. Some of you may have had a mother or grandmother who would can or store peaches. They would purchase the peaches put them in a can and place them on the shelf for later use. We called this "canning". After a while, you would have a nice can of preserved peaches, to be enjoyed for later use.

The keywords here ladies are "for later use".  We have a lot of men that have absolutely no intentions on marrying you. They will date you for five or so many years then propose to you with no wedding date. Then we get excited because he proposed. Jesus Christ disciples got excited about casting out devils, but Jesus Christ told them they were excited about the wrong thing. He told them that they should be excited that their names had been written down in the Lambs book of life.  It's good that the devils were cast out.  It's good that he asked you to marry him but what you need to know is on what day will this be fulfilled?  Let me tell you something ladies, first, you don't let a man date you for five or so many years with no wedding date.  Dragging you alone like

Linus did his blanket. When a man proposes to you, he needs to have a date with the ring. You are not a can of preservatives. Don't let this man place you on a shelf and whenever he decides he's ready for marriage, he pulls you off the shelf. Let me say it again, engagement rings come with dates. The word engagement means to do something or go somewhere at a fixed time. Whenever we accept an engagement with no fixed time, we have just placed ourselves on the shelf for later use. I can't say this enough ladies. It doesn't take a man five, ten, or even fifteen years to know if he wants you for his wife. Now it may take him that long to sow his wild oats and take inventory of all his options. Men are hunters and conquerors. What they want they get and make it their own. I heard a man of God say something like this. He stated, "When a man wants a motorcycle, he will go get a license to drive one". "When a man wants to go hunting, he will go get a license to hunt." Even comes down to a dog. When a man purchases an expensive dog, he will go get a license to say that he is the owner of the dog. But for some reason, he can't decide on a date to get a license for you. Okay, I'll wait for that answer.

A man with no fixed time doesn't have your best interest at heart. He has no intentions of marrying you. Don't get excited about the wrong thing. When a man is serious about his love for you, he will present you with a ring and reasonable fixed time all on the same day. I have witnessed many women who have been engaged for many years. These women are cohabitating and having children with men all on a proposal. Ladies let me explain something to you, if you are good enough to do all the above; don't you think you are good enough to have a fixed date?  Stop wasting your life with men who have no intentions of marrying you.  Because we all know what happens to women who have given there all for many years to men with no fixed date. The man ends up dropping them like a hot cake for Sally Sue.  Sally Sue wasn't there when this man didn't have a job (she shouldn't have been) and Sally Sue didn't have any children from this man.  She shouldn't have spit out not one child because the proposal doesn't mean it's okay to start having sex.  You gave him everything with no fixed date just a promise. Now you are sad and mad because Jim Bob has left you and moved in with Sally Sue across the street.  You don't have to ever put yourself in that position ladies.  You have the right to require not only an engagement ring but also a fixed date. If he doesn't want to give you a wedding date, then on to the next man.

# 10

# The Pedophile

*A person male or female who is sexually attracted to children.*

We have discussed all types of men that we don't want to be married too from the angry man to the porn addict. I believe the actions and motives of this one, the pedophile, is more damaging than the others because of the amount of pain he leaves behind. When children are molested it can alter their lives forever. Children can't process being molested, raped, or fondled, wether this comes from a parent, relative, friend or a Pastor. They don't know how to speak about it or even tell someone that it is happening. Immediately they feel as if they have done something wrong. In some cases, they believe that what was done to them is alright because of the relationship with the offender. Ladies listen to me for a minute. There is a process that child predators put into action as soon as they meet you and your children. This process is called grooming. Grooming is the actions used to gain trust in a child and a parent with the future intent of molesting the child. Ladies when you meet a man, he has no business babysitting for you. You think that this man really cares about you because he is so willing to keep your children. You may even believe he is really the one because he pays for your daycare. He is grooming you.

He is breaking down your defenses and building up your trust so he can have access to your children. Boyfriends should not be buying your daughters underwear. Boyfriends should not be giving your children money and buying gifts in secret. This is inappropriate behavior. Children and teenagers love gifts and toys that is what they are supposed to like because they are adolescents. As a parent, as the protector of your children, you should be able to recognize inappropriate behavior when you see it. It is also inappropriate for a man to touch your daughter's breast and rub his or her private body parts. I had to include boys private body parts too because men are not only molesting girls, they are molesting boys too. Speaking of inappropriate behavior stop letting your daughters sit on men's laps. I know this may all sound a bit extreme, but you had better not just pray but you had better watch along with asking your children some questions. Sometimes we can believe that a man is all into us but if the truth be told that man isn't thinking about you. He is after your child. He is looking to gain your love and trust so he can have his way with your children. He is a pedophile, a man who desires to have sex with a child! Preferably the child is shy, one with low self-esteem. A child who is not so sure of themselves. Ladies it's not the homeless man hiding in the bushes who is desiring to have sex, your children. It's that well-dressed, educated, most love family friend or respected community leader who is really the culprit. If your children come to you and tells you that someone is making them feel uncomfortable, please believe them. Ask questions and please don't tell your children to keep his or her mouth shut. When we tell our children to keep quiet it begins the process of our children becoming very rebellious. We wonder why Sally Sue is so sexually permissive and why Billy Bob is always high on drugs. Could it be because as a child or teenager their mother met a man who has been molesting them since they were children?

Children are a gift from God. It is our responsibility to give them a safe and healthy environment to grow in so that they can become productive citizens. Single mothers I know things get hard sometimes and we all just want a little help. You had better make sure that the help you choose is sent from God above, because some help isn't always good help. Ladies beware of wolves who come dressed in sheep clothing.

Every man who proposes to you does not have your best interest at heart. He could really be after your children. If you let the desire and passion to be married blind you and you end up marrying a pedophile be ready for a failed marriage with major devastation.

# 11

# Stop Providing for a Man

A diamond ring, a Louis Vuitton handbag, a Hermes Birkin bag, a Mercedes-Benz Maybach, and a pair of red bottom heels. What do all these items have in common? If you said "Quality". You would be right. All these items are the crème de la crème, the best of the best, superlative and very expensive. One thing we can all agree on is that if you plan on purchasing any of these items you are going to need some "Do-re-mi" money. It doesn't matter how well spoken you may be or how nice you dress. The prices will not be compromised  Either you will pay the cost, or you can travel on down to your local "Grab-A Bag" where the pickings are innumerable.

When dating or considering a husband you got to see yourself as the crème de la crème, the best. You must know your worth. Don't be afraid to proclaim who you are. Never settle for less. Never lower your standards. When a man approaches you, he must come correct. When a person enters the Hermes Store you must have your ducks in a row because nobody is running any deals. There are no specials, no layaways, and no scratch-off tickets. You must enter correct and be ready to pay the price. Never let a man enter your space in life expecting you to support him. You are never to be his provider. You don't provide the home. You don't provide the car and you don't pay his bills while he goes off to school and get a degree. You don't have to struggle and lose what you have to support him. Never give your body and bear his children while he tries to get his life together.

There is nothing new under the sun. When I was a young woman dating, I thought it was okay to give a man my everything to help him. It is the same way today. I see so many young girls giving their time, money, and body to support a man who doesn't even value them enough to marry them. I want to abolish this way of thinking today. You should never accept a zero in your life and be the one to stand beside him to make him a ten. When he enters your life, he should already be a ten or at least a nine and a half. I really don't know where we have learned this pattern or behavior from, maybe our childhood. Did we watch our mothers take care of our fathers? Did we watch our mothers support their boyfriend? Something has happened in the part of the brain that records history and develops patterns, because we are so quick to provide for a man. To make this way of thinking even worse we feel guilty about not providing for a man.

Please listen to me clearly, it's only in marriage that you are to give your total support. It's only in a marriage that you are to cleave to a man not before. When you become one flesh then you give him your everything not while dating. A man will never come to take from you. A man will never lay back and let you support him. A man will never take from you and your children. He will never watch you suffer at his expense, NEVER. You want to know why? Well, it's because God has wired a man to be the head, the provider, the protector and when a man finds himself doing anything other than this, the man immediately becomes what we in the south like to call a "jelly back". This is a man who doesn't have the backbone to stand up and be a man. In other words when a woman must take care of a man, he becomes emasculated.

Ladies and young girls with all your understanding please understand this. You always deserve to be treated well and cared for. You should never be taking care of a man. A man who has laid down his toys and picked up his manhood will take joy in providing and protecting you. It will be the very air he breathes. It will be his reason for laboring as hard as he does. So, ladies, when the man steps into your Hemes store of life talking about, he wants to date or marry you make sure he has considered the cost because no sales is going on. There will be no red-light specials and we will not be providing for the purchase. If he decides the price is too high send him on down to the "Grab-A Bag" and maintain your crème de la cremes.

# 12

# Mr. Right

We have discussed so many types of men, from the abusive man all the way down to the man who expects a woman to provide for him. I can even remember when the "church mothers" would say, "baby you don't need a man, all you need is Jesus Christ let him be your husband".

I'm going to keep this as simple as possible. People are foundations. If you choose to marry a man who is abusive crazy, unfaithful, lazy, no work ethics who has inappropriate relationships with children, have been emasculated and disrespects his mother, you can then expect your marriage to be filled with damages, cracks and over time sinking.  If you choose to marry a man, Mr. Right, that would never a raise a hand to hurt you, that has a reasonable right portion of his mind, who believes in providing for his family, who would never bring shame to dishonor your vowels, that loves his mama along with honoring God.  You will have just chosen someone that is going to increase the durability of your marriage remaining and withstanding over time.

You have a clean slate ladies. You can determine what type of man you want for a husband and what type of man you want to father your children.  This is your decision.  I tell women all the time if you chose to have children from a man that refuses to pay his child support and be involved with his children's life that is danger. What about when he takes care of Sally Sues children but not his own? Guess what? That is who you chose. Stop all that fussing and choose Mr. Right the next time.

We have got to see beyond "right now", how he makes me feel, the car he drives, how good he smells, his eyes are green, and he has a six pack. Baby overtime them eyes are going to turn bad, and his six-pack is going to turn into a no-pack. All this outward beauty fades. It can't be the determining factor for marriage. You must choose Mr. Right for the long haul, because after the honeymoon life happens and the challenges will begin. When you get older; is he is going to trade you in for a younger woman? If you get sick or in an accident is, he going to leave you? If he loses his job; is he going to give up and become dependent on you? If you have children; is he going to touch them inappropriately?  Will his character allow him to say no to another woman in private because he remembers he has a wife?  Mr. Right is not perfect, but his foundation is sure, and it will protect the people inside.  I know the divorce rate is high, but we don't have to be a part of the statistic.  I believe we can all experience the joys of a healthy marriage and never end up marrying the WRONG MAN.

Women young and old it's okay to have a standard.  It's okay to want the best and seek excellence.  It's okay for you to not have children from a man who doesn't want to marry you.  It's okay to be a virgin.  It's okay to not play house and become submissive to a man that's not willing to give you his last name.  It's okay for you to not be with a man who gets high, who wears his pants off his behind who dropped out of school who has multiple women who is verbally abusive. It's okay to have standards and say no to unqualified men with a smile. Let folk say what they want to say about, "She thinks she's pretty." "She thinks she's too good." Baby, do you think Meghan Markie considered what people thought or said about her? I think not, because her address is at the palace and she is the wife of the Prince. I had to put that in there because people will try to make you feel like something is wrong with you have discovered your worth. You have chosen not to marry an ordinary man and live in dysfunction.

In my closing, I would say that it has brought me great joy to know that so many of you will begin to make better choices when choosing men to date and eventually marry. I believe that the murder rate of women being killed by their husbands and the rate of women being abandon will come an all time low.  No more fear and no more settling will be in the hearts and minds of women everywhere.  From the rich house to the poor house we can boldly declare that we will not MARRY THE WRONG MAN!

# About the Author

Yvette Hayes is the daughter of William Douglas Hayes and the late Lynn Mckoy Hayes, the step daughter of Mrs. Mary Hayes. Yvette is the proud mother of two children Shalonda Nicole Shotwell and Antonio Pierre Brown, Jr. The grandmother of one lovely granddaughter Danella Janay Harvey aka "NannaBread" and one grandson Dillion Pierre Brown. One sister Connie Hayes and two brothers Willie D. parker and the late Kenny Mckoy. She serves as an Evangelist at the New Light Apostolic Church of Jesus Christ under the leadership of Pastor Bobbie Todd. Her passion is that souls will be saved, and women will know that they matter. Her favorite scripture is *Philippians 1:6.*

To contact Yvette Hayes email:

YvetteHayesNC47@gmail.com

Made in the USA
Middletown, DE
21 January 2023

22764179R00064